My
Phonics
Workbook

This book belongs to:

Way to Go!

After completing each activity, color a star to track how much you've done!

1 2 3 4

5 6 7 8 9 10

11 12 13 14 15 16

17 18 19 20 21 22

23 24 25 26 27 28

29	30	31	32	33	34
35	36	37	38	39	40
41	42	43	44	45	46
47	48	49	50	51	52
53	54	55	56	57	58
59	60	61	62	63	64
65	66	67	68	69	70

71	72	73	74	75	76
77	78	79	80	81	82
83	84	85	86	87	88
89	90	91	92	93	94
95	96	97	98	99	100
101					

My Phonics Workbook

101
Games and Activities to Support Reading Skills

LAURIN BRAINARD

Illustrations by Robin Boyer

ROCKRIDGE PRESS

Interior Designer: Liz Cosgrove
Cover Designer: Stephanie Sumulong
Photo Art Director: Sue Bischofberger
Editor: Jeanine Le Ny
Production Editor: Andrew Yackira
Photography: Author photograph by Brooke Bakken Photography
Illustrations © Robin Boyer, 2019.

ISBN: Print 978-1-64152-441-4

Note to Parents

Hello! Welcome to *My Phonics Workbook*, a fun and interactive way to introduce your preschooler to the world of letters and their sounds. This book is designed for children ages 4 to 6 to help them build the pre-reading skills they will need for kindergarten! The games and activities in this book are designed to keep your child entertained, while reinforcing phonics skills that help teach children how to read. As a first-grade teacher and mom of preschoolers, I have personally seen and shared in the excitement a child experiences when first learning to read!

The activities in this book gradually increase in difficulty. Completing the easiest activities first will help your child feel confident and motivated to keep going. First your child will be introduced to the letters A to Z and then will move on to blends and digraphs. Begin each activity by reading the directions aloud to your child. For each letter of the alphabet, start by saying the name of the letter and directing your child to trace the letter. Then guide your child in all activities, such as drawing a line through a maze or circling objects on a page. You can also show your child how to circle, trace, and write by using your finger before your child begins to write on the pages.

Be sure to go through the book at your child's pace. You will know when your child is ready for an activity if they are excited and want to continue working through the book. An uneager or struggling child is a sign that an activity may be too difficult for now. If this happens, either offer more help, or wait until the child is a bit older to move ahead. Learning is fluid, and what is too hard today may become easier to master in the near future.

Young children learn best when the material is fun, and the games and activities in this book were intended for just that. I hope you enjoy working with and watching your little one having fun, lighting up with each achievement, and, most of all, loving learning!

Let's get started!

Laurin

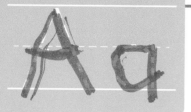

1. A Is for Apple

This is the letter **A**. Say the name of each picture. Then circle the ones that begin with the **a** sound.

2. Amy Picks Apples

Color the (A) red. Color the (a) green.

3. Adam Ant

It's time for dinner! Follow the path to show Adam the way home.

4. Busy, Buzzy Bee

Trace the bee's trail. Then circle all the foods that begin with the **b** sound.

5. Billy Buys Balloons

Place an X on all the balloons with the letter **B**.

6. Colorful Caterpillar

Color the cute caterpillar. Use as many colors as you can!

7. What Begins with C?

Draw a line from the letter C to each picture that begins with the c sound.

8. C Is for Candle

Today is Conner's birthday! Draw **5** candles on the cake so he can make a wish.

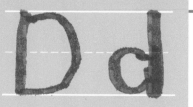

9. In the Doghouse!

Follow the **d** sounds to help Daisy Dog reach her home.

10. Duck Dives

Find and color each letter D.

11. Dancing Dolphins

Color the dolphins. Then get up and dance like one!

12. Ella Elephant

E is Ella's favorite letter! Put a ✔ on the objects that begin with the **e** sound.

13. Lost Elk

Follow the letter **E** to help Eddie Elk get back to the forest.

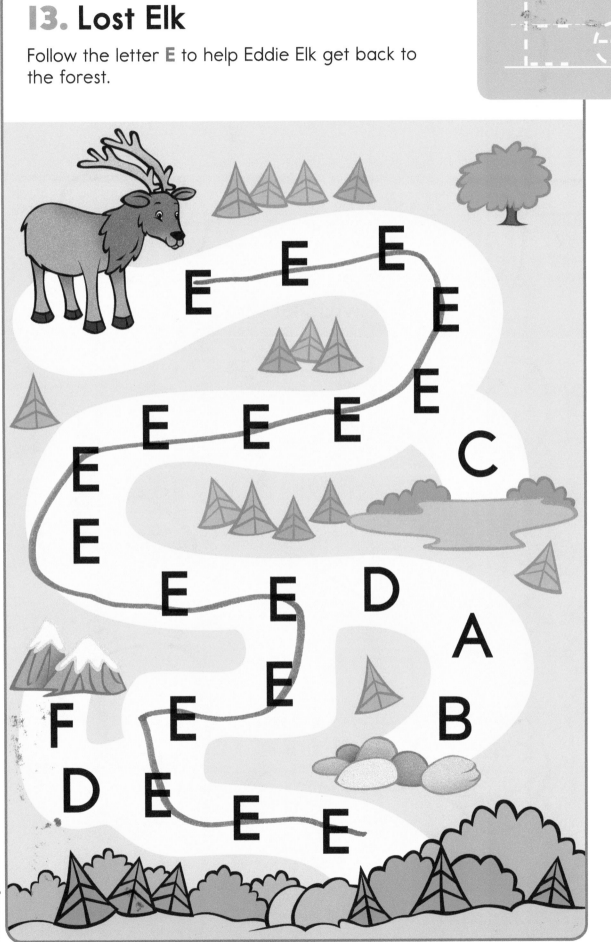

14. Fish Friends

Fred the fish has lots of friends. Color the fish whose names begin with the **f** sound.

Fabio

Fernanda

Madison

Pat

Francis

Bill

Fabian

Noah

Felipe

Frankie

15. Word Hunt

Find and circle these **4** words that are inside the flower.

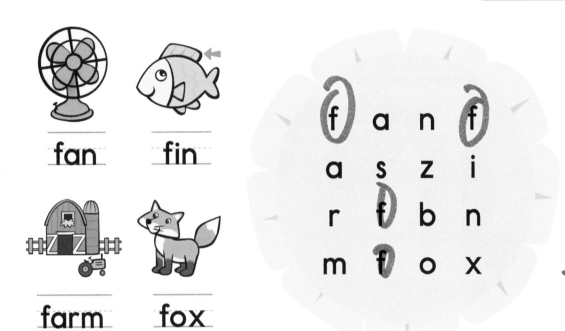

fan   fin

farm   fox

f a n f
a s z i
r f b n
m f o x

16. Visit Fun City

Fun City is filled with things that begin with the **f** sound. How many can you find?

17. Gorilla Grows Grapes

Draw a line from each  G and each g to the matching basket.

18. Great Gifts!

Color the pictures that begin with the **g** sound. Then draw a line from each gift to the correct box.

19. Gumball Machine

Color the gumballs with pictures of things that end with the **g** sound.

20. Hay Is for Horses

Find and circle the thing that makes each horse a little different from the others.

21. A Hidden Message!

Color each **H** and **h** to see a secret message.

f	H	N	O	h	j	w	U	I
a	H	z	f	h	E	H	N	V
R	h	B	Z	H	k	y	r	W
M	h	H	h	h	n	h	d	C
T	H	A	u	H	i	H	P	s
g	h	n	E	H	J	h	z	k
J	h	m	k	H	S	h	w	R

22. Henry Hunts for H Words

Draw a box around **5** things that begin with the **h** sound.

23. I Is For . . .

Color each **I** brown and each **i** pink to find a yummy treat!

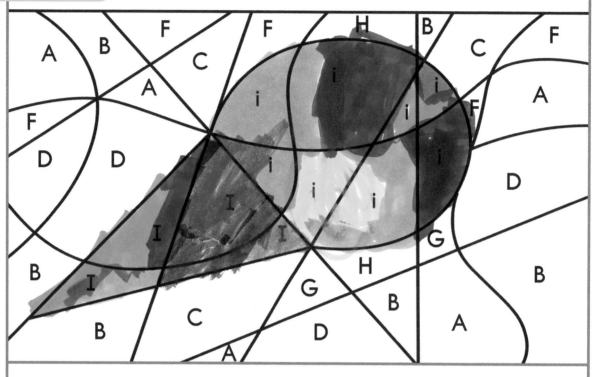

24. Ivan on the Ice

Which path leads to Ivan's ice skates?

25. Inside Iguana's Bedroom

Can you spot the **5** things that are different in these pictures?

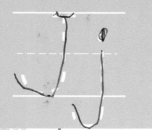

26. Connect to J

Connect the dots from **A** to **J** to see who is floating in the ocean.

27. Jackrabbit Jumps for Joy

Help the jackrabbit jump to all the things that begin with the **j** sound.

28. Kangaroo Class

Write the letter **k** at the beginning of each word.

Koala

Key

Kiwi

Karate

Kitten

Kayak

28

29. Kids with Kites

Draw a line to connect each kid to the matching kite.

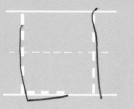

30. Lizard's Lawn Sale

What's for sale? All the items that begin with an **L** sound are! Find and circle them.

30

31. Lion's Lunch

Lucky Lion eats only foods that begin with the **L** sound. Put an **X** on the items that Lucky does NOT eat.

32. What a Mess!

Can you find **4** objects that begin with the **m** sound that don't belong in the ocean? Draw them in the mermaid's net.

33. On the Moon

Find and circle the **10** letter **M**s hidden in the picture.

Mm

34. Mangoes for Monkeys

Trace the lines from **M** to **m** so the monkeys can eat mangoes!

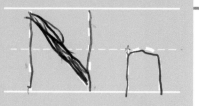

35. Nightingale's Nest

Follow the letter **N** to get the nightingale to her nest.

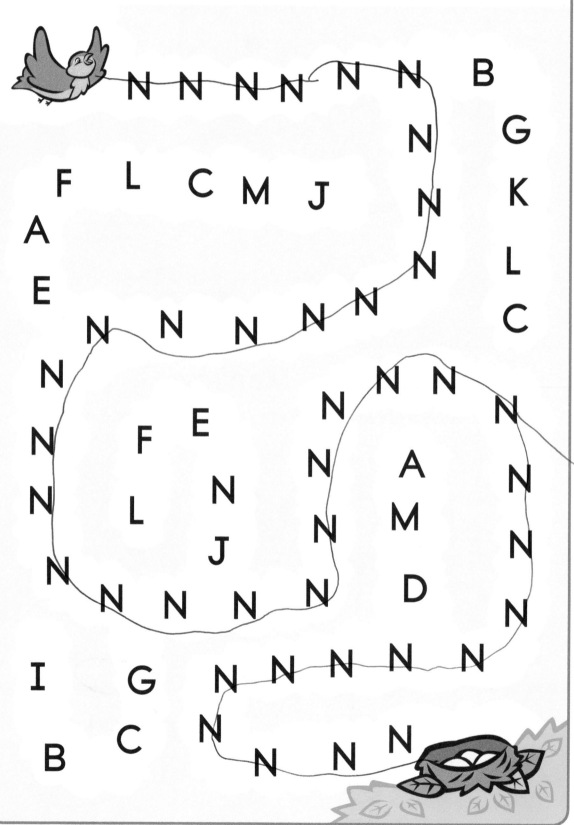

36. Nice Nancy

Nancy needs: nuts, noodles, a newspaper, and nachos. Find and circle each one.

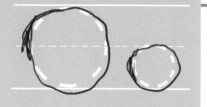

37. Oranges for Oscar

Show Oscar the path to his snack. Color in each box with the letter O or o.

38. Ollie Octopus!

Help Ollie add the letter o to the right place in each word, okay?

l o g

c o rn

39. O Word Search

Find and draw a line through each word hidden in the puzzle below.

oatmeal   olive   orchid   omelet

ocean   octopus   ostrich

o	o	r	c	h	i	d	s	o
a	b	o	o	l	i	v	e	c
t	z	s	a	x	d	o	m	t
m	l	t	o	f	k	m	y	o
e	n	r	c	w	a	e	g	p
a	r	i	e	t	m	l	c	u
l	b	c	a	d	m	e	k	s
b	g	h	n	v	p	t	o	n

40. Princess Pia's Play

Princess Pia needs you to color everything that begins with the **p** sound. Pretty please!

parrot · panda · pigeon · puppet · plane · police officer · paintbrush

38

41. Penguin Race!

Which penguin will reach the popsicle stand first?
Find and color the shortest path to see!

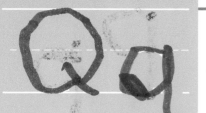

42. Quilt for a Queen

Write the next letter in the pattern in each row to complete the quilt.

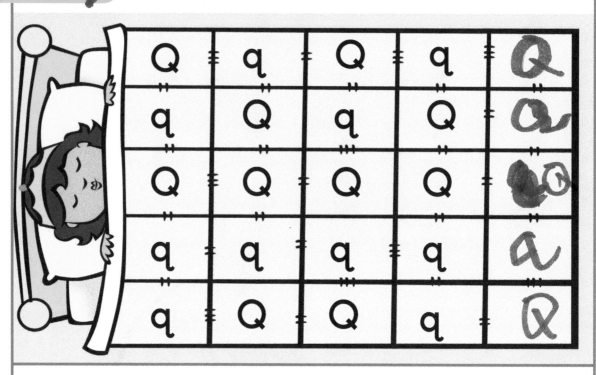

Q	q	Q	q	Q
q	Q	q	Q	a
Q	Q	Q	Q	
q	q	q	q	a
q	Q	Q	q	R

43. Quality Quails

Circle each word in the story that begins with the letter **Q** or **q**. Color the picture.

Quinn was a quiet quail. He quite liked to write. Using a quill pen, he wrote about Quentin the quarterback. He used a whole quart of ink!

GO QUAILS

44. The Question Is . . .

What is hidden in the picture below? Color each space with the letter **Q** or **q** to find out!

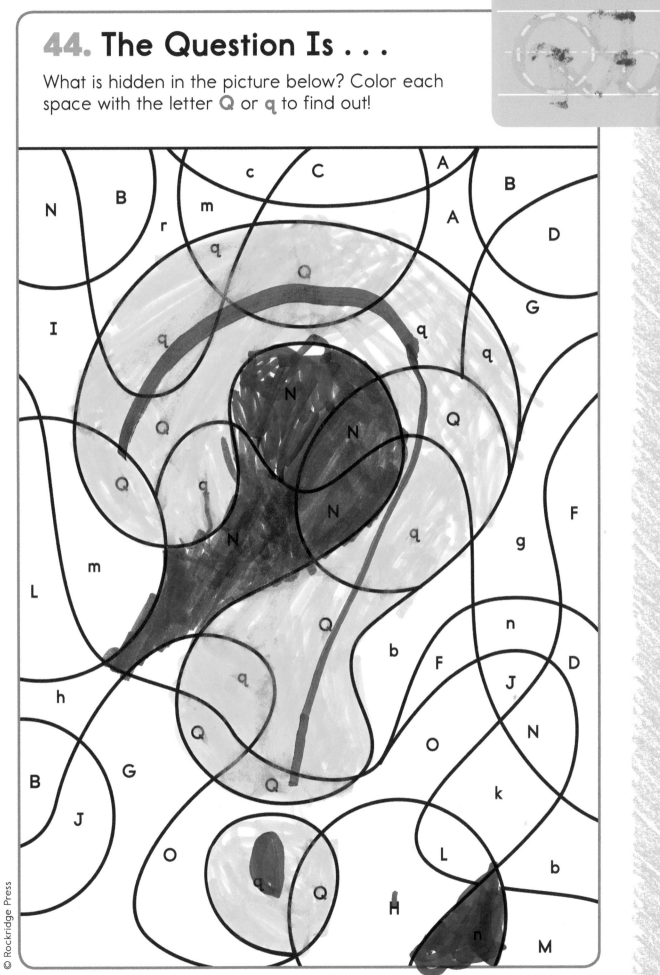

45. Ready for Raymond?

Connect the dots from **A** to **R** to meet Raymond. Be ready to color in your new friend!

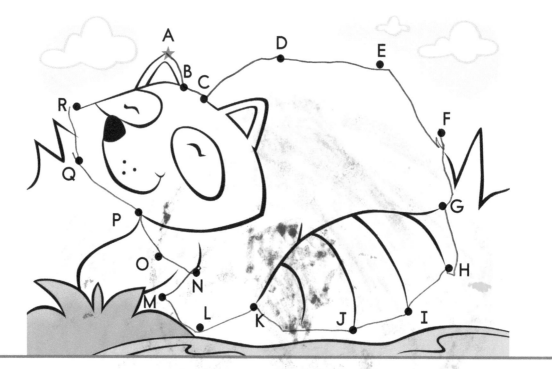

46. Make These Words Right

Unscramble the words and write them in the boxes.

urg

r	u	g

art

r	a	t

arm

r	a	m

dro

r	o	d

47. Robot Rescue

Rob Robot needs you to draw the rest of him. Use the left side of Rob as a guide to draw his right side.

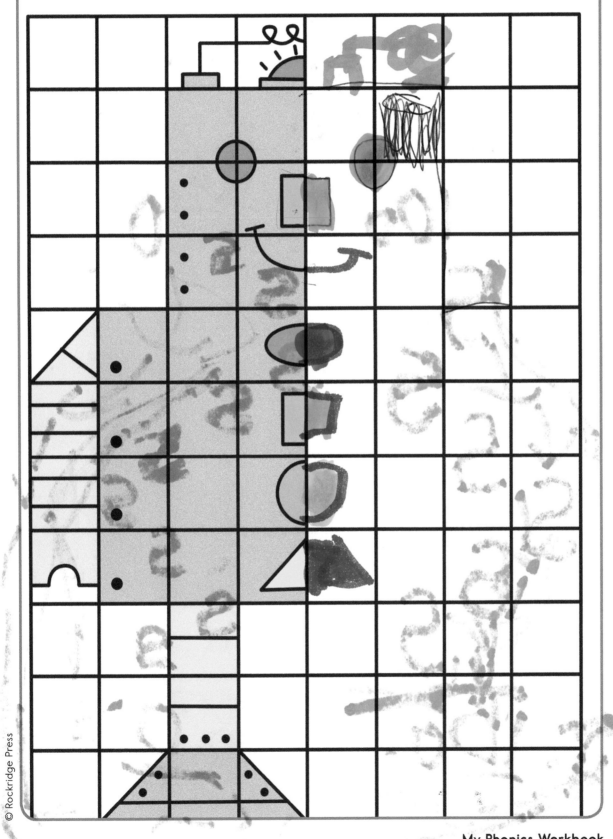

My Phonics Workbook **43**

© Rockridge Press

48. Skunk and Squirrel

Skunk and Squirrel are super speedy! How quickly can you trace the letters?

My Phonics Workbook

49. See and Say S Words

Point to each object and say its name. How many begin with the **s** sound?

I found _____ things that begin with the **s** sound.

50. Time to Color!

Use the guide below to color the picture. Can you guess what will appear?

51. Let's Travel!

There are **4** transportation words beginning with **T** in the picture below. Find and circle each letter **T**.

52. Tiger's Trail

Find and color all the things that begin with the **t** sound.

53. Umpires and Umbrellas

Trace the lines between the umpires and their umbrellas.

54. What Starts with U?

Draw a line to match each picture to its word.

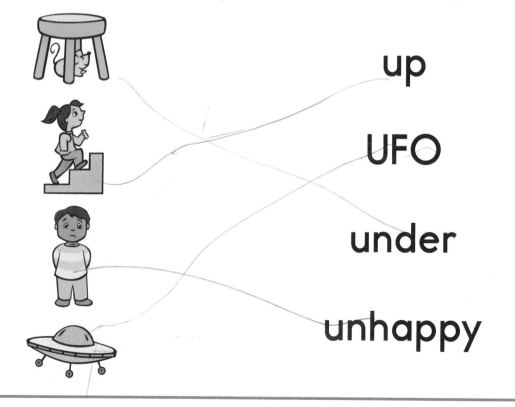

up

UFO

under

unhappy

55. Ursula Unpacks

Find and circle all the items in the picture that begin with the letter **U**.

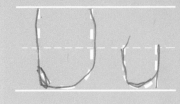

56. Vicky's Vacation

Follow the pictures that begin with the **v** sound to help Vicky find the van.

57. Very Good!

Place an X on the pictures that do NOT begin with the **v** sound.

58. Happy Valentine's Day!

Trace the Valentine below and decide who you would give it to. Then color it very bright **red**!

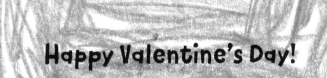

Dear Mum

Happy Valentine's Day!

From ANPLIQUE

59. What Appears?

Color each space with an object that begins with the **w** sound.

60. Words Wanted!

Can you finish this crossword puzzle? Use the word bank and the picture clues to help you write the correct words.

Word Bank
wet   watermelon
wand   web   wasp

61. What Ends with X?

Circle the pictures that end with the **x** sound.

box

bowl

six

quail

backpack

mix

fox

mailbox

62. X is for X-ray

On the screen below, draw what you think an X-ray of this dog might look like.

63. Fix the Xylophone

Fill in the missing letters on the Xylophone. Then write the letters in order in the space below. What do they spell?

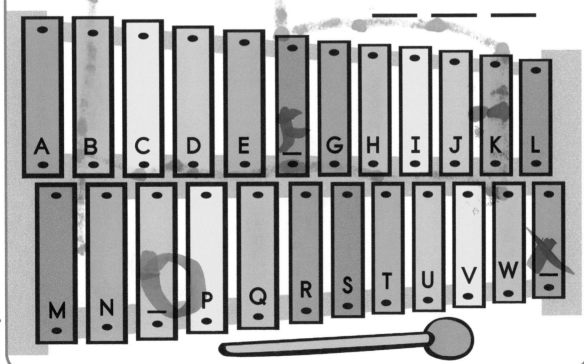

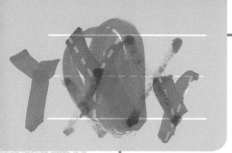

64. Yak's Yacht

Follow the letters, from **A** to **Y**, to help Yak reach his yacht.

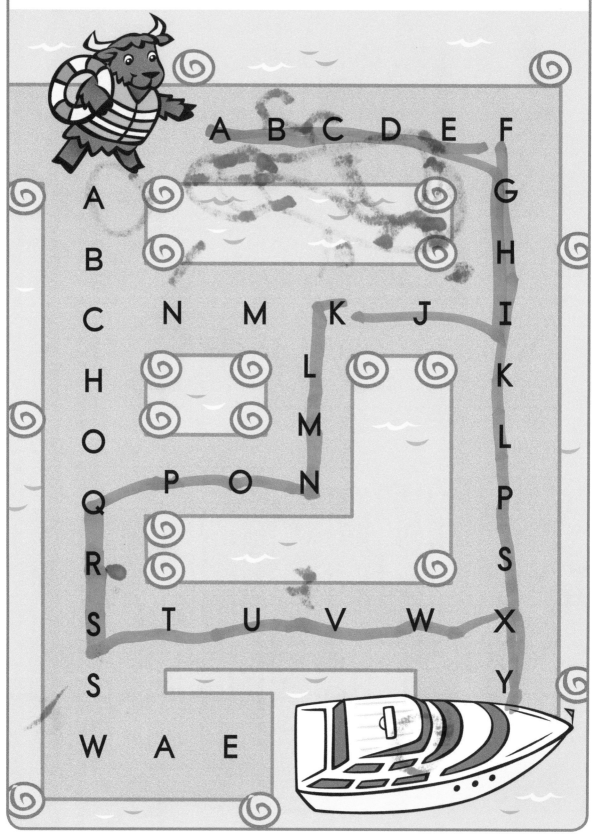

My Phonics Workbook

65. You Find the Y Words!

Find and circle each **Y** word in the puzzle below.

Word Bank

yak   yard   yogurt
yam   yawn   yarn

66. Z Is For . . .

Connect the dots from **A** to **Z**. Which animal do you see?

67. Zip!

Read and trace the sentence below. Then color the picture.

Zack zips

his zipper.

68. From A to Zoo

Write the first letter of each animal's name in the space below.
Then put a circle around your favorite!

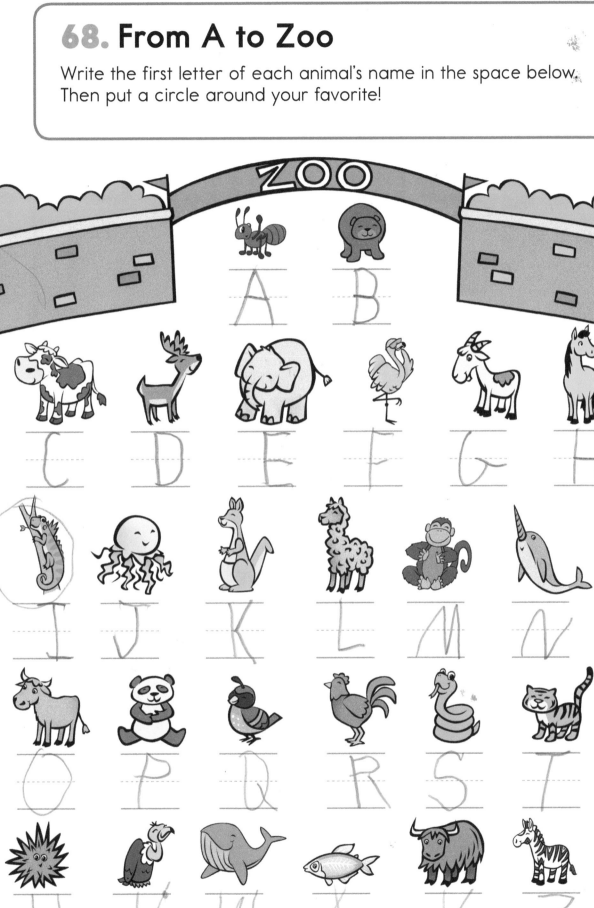

69. Let's Learn Vowels (A, E, I, O, U)

Say the name of the picture. Listen for the first sound in the word. Then use the guide to color the pictures.

70. It's a Match!

Circle the word that matches each picture.

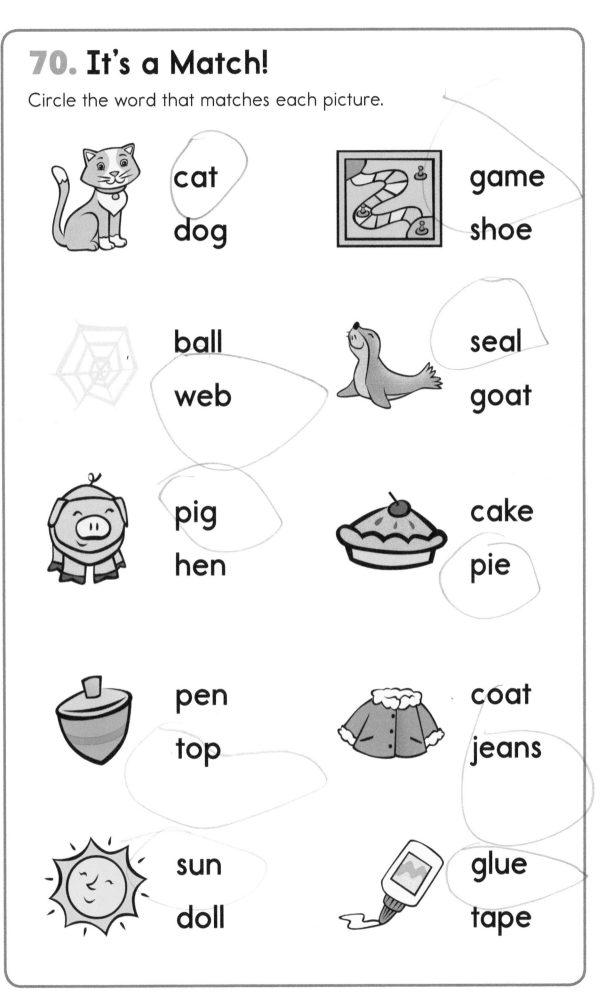

cat
dog

game
shoe

ball
web

seal
goat

pig
hen

cake
pie

pen
top

coat
jeans

sun
doll

glue
tape

71. Blue Blanket

Find and circle **4** objects on the blue blanket that begin with the **bl** sound.

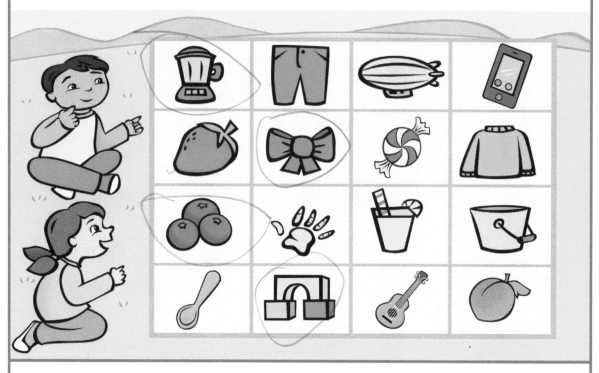

72. Flamingo's Flip-Flops

Help Flamingo find her flip-flops. Color the boxes with words that begin with the **fl** sound.

floss	play	plot	plump	dry
float	flick	gloss	slid	black
clay	flag	flower	flute	slab
drop	grow	slant	flippers	flame

73. The Clock Is Ticking!

Help Clara find the things that begin with the **cl** sound before the clock runs out!

74. Gl Sounds!

Grab a friend, and take turns coloring in the pictures below. The first one to color **3** pictures in a row wins!

glasses

glove

globe

glue

glow

glad

glass

glide

gladiator

75. Plato Is . . .

What kind of animal is Plato? Use the code below to find out.

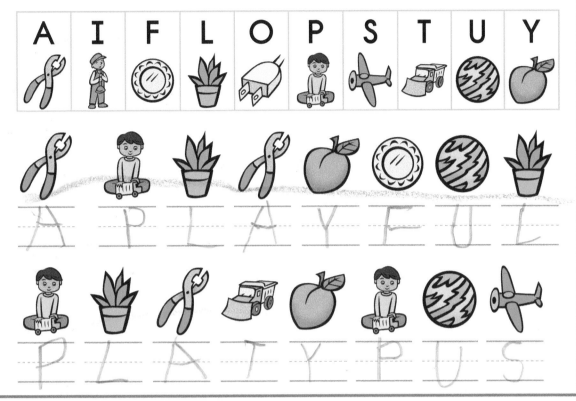

A	I	F	L	O	P	S	T	U	Y

A PLAYFUL

PLATYPUS

76. Sloan and Slaney's Adventure

Draw a line in one color from Sloan to the sled. Draw a line in another color from Slaney to the sleigh.

77. I Can Blend

Say the name of the picture. Listen for the blend in the word. Then use the guide to color the pictures.

My Phonics Workbook

Help Bree add the **br** blend to the beginning of each word.

broom

brownies

bread

broccoli

brown

brush

79. Dress the Dragon

This dragon is dreaming of a pretty dress. What do you think it looks like?

80. Gracie Groundhog

Gracie grabs everything that begins with the **gr** sound. Find and circle all the things Gracie would like to grab.

81. Presenting Pr Words

Fill in the missing letters of each word to complete the crossword puzzle. Use the pictures as clues.

82. Try This!

Color each square using the color key, and see what you create that starts with the **tr** sound.

83. R-Blends

Say the names of the pictures. Then circle the blend that begins each word.

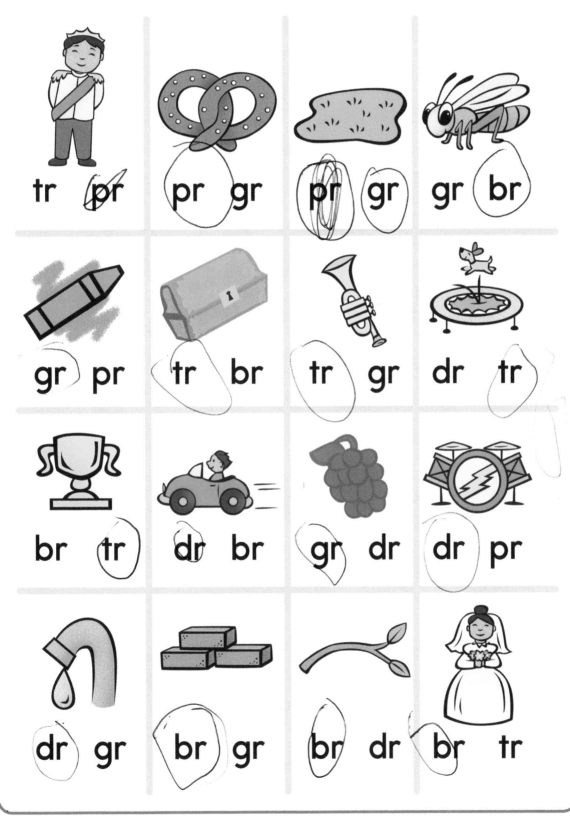

tr   pr   pr   gr   pr   gr   gr   br

gr   pr   tr   br   tr   gr   dr   tr

br   tr   dr   br   gr   dr   dr   pr

dr   gr   br   gr   br   dr   br   tr

84. Two Scoops, Please!

Which sundaes belong to kids whose names begin with the **sc** sound? Draw each one an extra scoop of ice cream!

| Scarlett | Scott | Sara | Scout | Sam | Sonjia |

85. Skunk's Skates

Help Skunk reach the skates. Color each box with the **sk** sound.

sky	small	swift	slam	spin	stage
skate	skunk	skill	skin	spout	sum
swim	six	smoke	ski	skid	skit
storm	swell	steam	sweat	stop	skillet

My Phonics Workbook

86. One Sweet Town

Color the words on the path that begin with the **sw** sound. Then color the rest of the picture.

sweet
shell
swing
swim
shift
swan
shoes
skate
swat
sweep

87. Snap to It!

Draw a line to match each word to its picture. Then color the pictures.

snake

snowman

sneakers

snail

My Phonics Workbook

88. Spider Spins Webs

Circle the webs with words that begin with the **sp** sound.

spaghetti

spoon

snowflake

shirt

skates

star

shark

stop sign

sponge

89. Stanley Starfish's Puzzle

Stanley has hidden words that begin with the **st** sound in the puzzle below. Can you find them? Be sure to look across, down, and diagonally.

s	r	q	v	s	t	u	d	y
t	l	s	t	a	i	r	s	z
o	x	s	h	s	t	a	m	p
p	s	b	t	g	j	k	n	s
m	t	a	r	o	z	e	v	t
l	o	c	g	d	n	h	x	a
s	o	i	o	r	a	e	b	g
t	l	g	s	t	e	m	p	e

stop ✓ study ✓ stage ✓ stone stool

stem stamp stairs

90. All Blended Up

Use the blends in the blender to complete the words.

st   sc
sk   sw
sp   sn

s**k**irt

s**w**eep

s**t**ar

s**c**arf

s**p**oon

s**n**orkel

91. Stroll Through This One

Can you find **8** words that start with the **str** sound? Be sure to look across, down and diagonally.

strap

straw

stream

strong

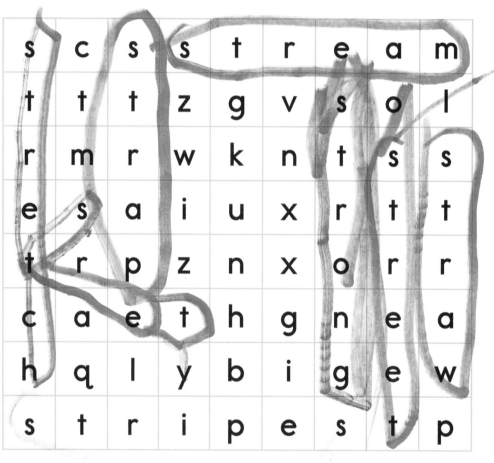

s	c	s	s	t	r	e	a	m
t	t	t	z	g	v	s	o	l
r	m	r	w	k	n	t	s	s
e	s	a	i	u	x	r	t	t
t	r	p	z	n	x	o	r	r
c	a	e	t	h	g	n	e	a
h	q	l	y	b	i	g	e	w
s	t	r	i	p	e	s	t	p

street

stretch

string

stripes

92. Splashing Is Splendid!

Help the boy find his umbrella. Splash through the puddles with words that begin with the **spl** sound.

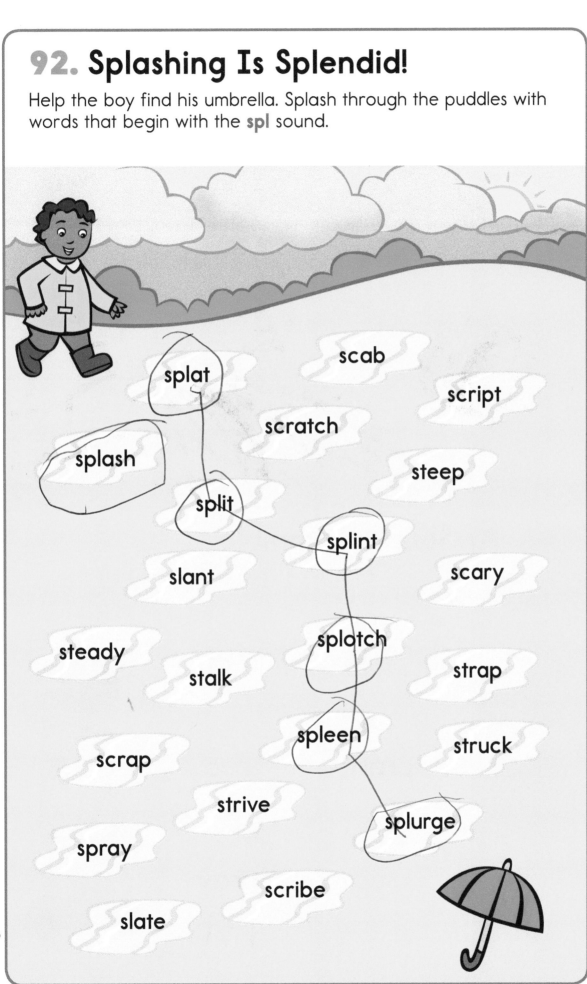

splat

scab

script

scratch

splash

steep

split

splint

slant

scary

steady

splotch

strap

stalk

scrap

spleen

struck

strive

splurge

spray

scribe

slate

93. Orange Picking

Circle the words with the **or** sound. Draw these words in the picture below.

orange

pineapple

sun

fork

girl

storm

horn

rainbow

94. Ar Sound Scramble

Unscramble and write each word. Then draw a line from the word to the matching picture.

narb

narb

raj

raj

prah

Prah

rac

rac

krba

Krba

nray

nray

95. Pop Goes the Word

Say each word. Listen for the middle sound. Then write the word next to the bucket of popcorn with the same sound.

term   fern   surf
turn   curl   stir
firm   dirt   verb

er — verb   fern   term

ir — dirt   stir   firm

ur — curl   turn   curl

96. Sheldon and Shawna

Use the word bank to help you finish the story.

Word Bank

sheep   shoes   shiny   Shark   shopper   shops

Sheldon _____ is a _____

He _____ for things like _____

for Shawna the _____ .

Shawna likes her shoes _____ .

97. Cheese, Please!

Get Charlie Mouse to the cheese in the center of the maze. He'll need to pass objects that begin with the **ch** sound to get there!

98. What Ends with Th?

Color the pictures that end with the **th** sound.

My Phonics Workbook

99. Whale Writing

Can you help this whale write **3** words that begin with the **wh** sound?

___istle

___iskers

___eelbarrow

Now, unscramble the letters below to see the whale's favorite color.

thewi

_____

Here's a clue: it's the same color as snow.

100. Show Some Thinking

Complete the words in the puzzle. Use the numbered pictures as clues.

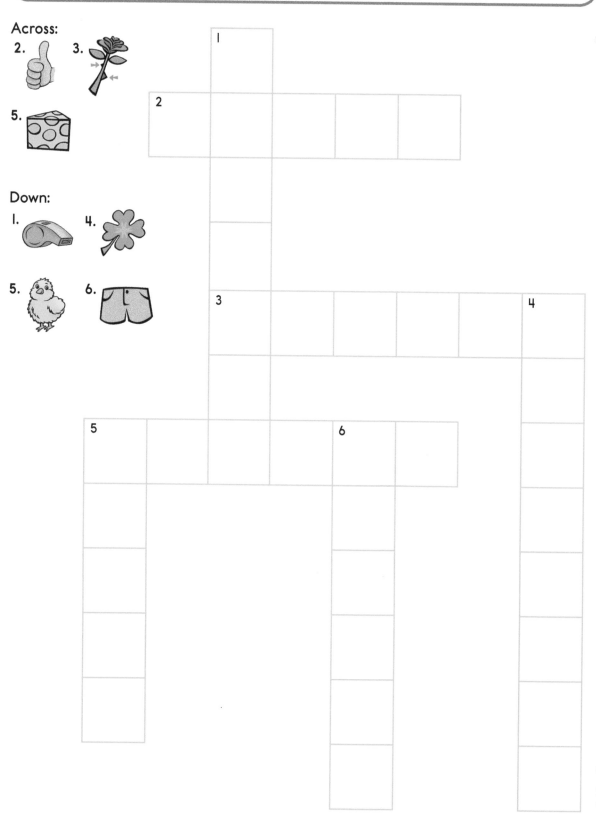

Across:
2.
3.
5.

Down:
1.
4.
5.
6.

My Phonics Workbook

101. On Your Way!

Use the code below to find out what you can do next!

Answer Key

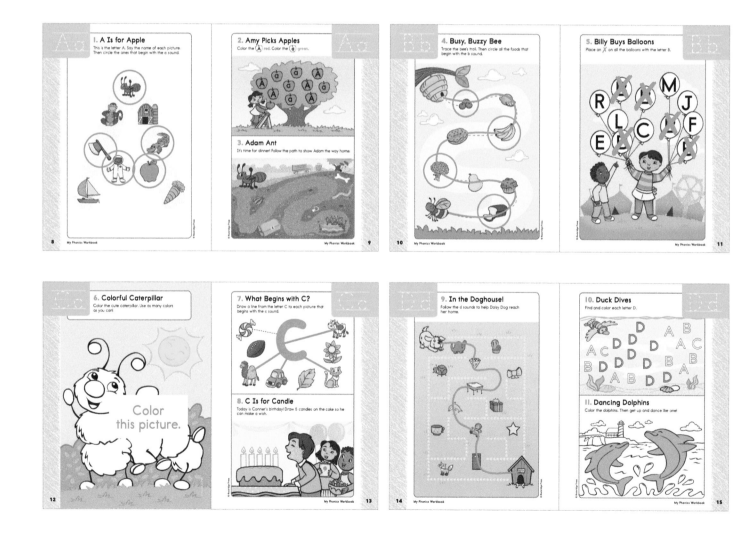

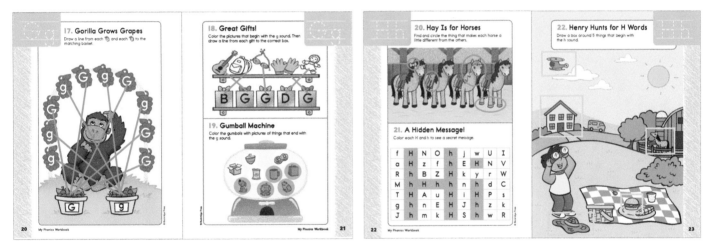

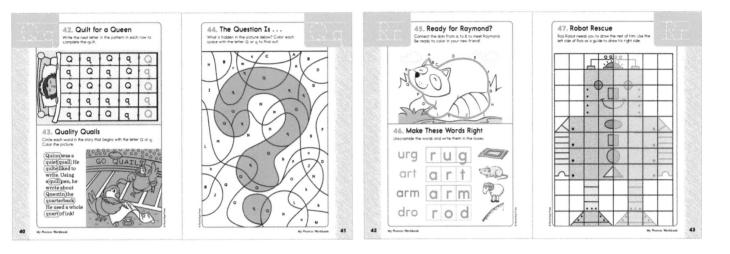

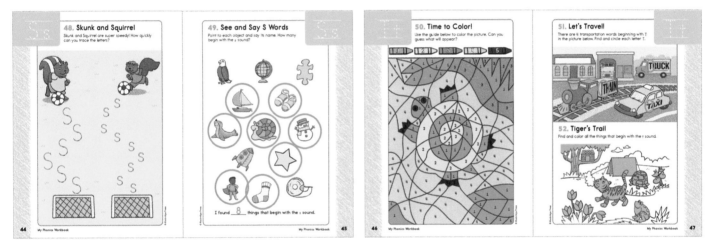

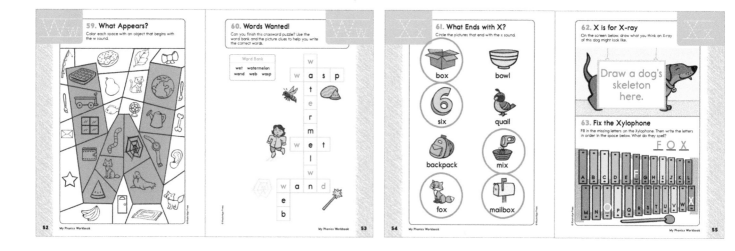

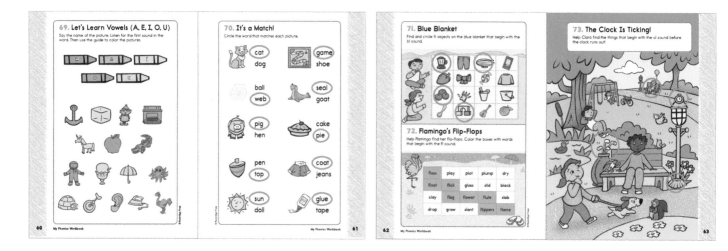

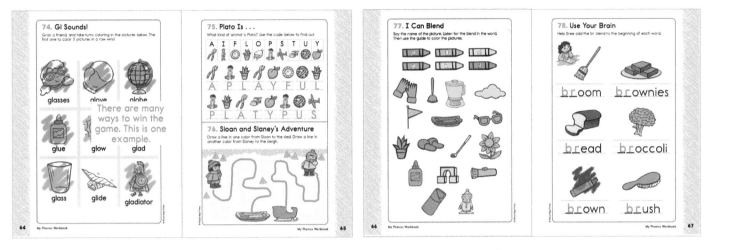

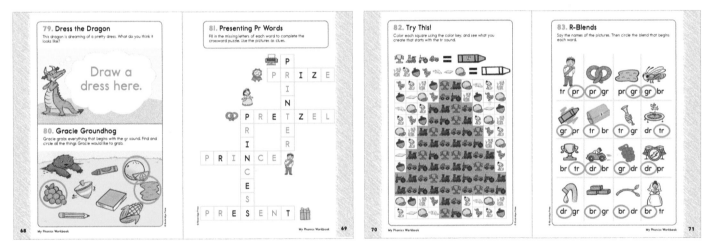

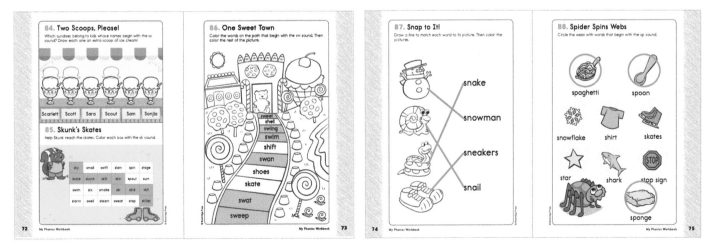

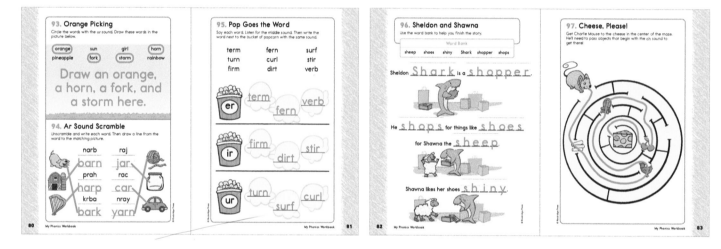

Index

About the Author

 Laurin Brainard, M.Ed., is the founder of and curriculum designer for The Primary Brain (ThePrimaryBrain.com). Through her blog, Laurin shares preschool ideas, fun activities including crafts, and teaching tips. Laurin is also a mom to preschoolers and a first-grade teacher. When she isn't teaching or designing children's resources, Laurin enjoys playing and making memories with her family.

CONGRATULATIONS!

You are on your way to becoming a reader!

_____

(your name)

has completed all the activities in

My Phonics Workbook.

YOU'RE A PHONICS ALL-STAR!

9 781641 524414